Ready set Bail:
A guide to navigating the pitfalls of bail

A. Chance Duncan

Why Did I Write This Book?

I wrote this book for the many defendants that have to deal with legal matters across the United States. The criminal justice system is very challenging and very political. It is important that when facing legal issues, that you have some guide or some advice or direction. It is also important that when going through the process, which are at times lengthy, that you are fully informed and fully aware. Being informed and being aware can save you time, money, and even your health. Enjoy this read.

Meet The Author

A aron Duncan is a native of Cleveland, Ohio. After serving honorably in the United States Marine Corps, Mr. Duncan accrued twelve years of experience owning and operating a bail bond service. To date, he has helped 17,000 clients to secure their freedom, and in the course of his duties he has observed over 30,000 motions and trials.

Mr. Duncan has helped to train, develop and license more than 25 bail agents. He is also a proud member of Professional Bail Agents of the United States.

For more information on bail bonding, and assistance with the bail bond process, please call 1-877-787-3380, or visit www.chancesbailbonds.com or you can visit the author's personal site, Callchance4bail.com

Table Of Content

The True Meaning of Your John Hancock

A bail bond is a document in which a prisoner and one or more sureties guarantee that the prisoner will attend the court hearing of the charge against him if he is released on bail. Most people posting bail for someone, have no clue or idea what kind of documents they are to sign. They end up rushing or moving fast to get their loved one out of jail. It's not that easy. You have to take time to recognize what you're signing, and what kind of contract you're entering into with either the courts or the bail bondsman.

Read This Before You Talk to a Bail Bondsman

I t is Important that you are aware when posting a Bail Bond, what kind of Bond you need executed. In the legal system you have different types of bonds. Some are civil and some are Criminal. Often times people get confused on exactly what they need to do. Some bonds are traditionally called cash or corporate surety bonds. These bonds are posted in the form of cash (US currency), which is a licensed bail entity for that particular state or jurisdiction.

We also have what is called **appeal bonds**. These are bonds that can be posted in the same form as appealing cases to higher courts.

There are the **child support bonds**. Bail bondsmen do not traditionally post this kind of bond. They are required to be paid in cash to the social services or child support enforcement division. Many times defendants are held in jail having to pay a significant amount for child support, and that fee cannot be arranged through bondsmen. If it is, a lawyer will be hired, and motion is put before the court to have those conditions changed or adjusted.

There are also **personal bonds**. These do not require posting any monetary funds, only a promise, on your own "personal recognizance" to appear in court on the appointed date.

Immigration bonds is another type of bond. Immigration bonds are immigration and custom enforcement bonds. These are bonds that are federally posted with the ICE office. They are not traditionally posted like a regular bail bond. Sometimes arrangements have to be in full cash collateral, or they may have to be posted through a bail bondsman who may set certain conditions.

Federal bonds. Federal bonds are different types of bonds. These bonds are riskier and sometimes there may be hearing when cash and monies that are posted by the defendant have to be verified where their source is from. Understanding the bonds that may be set is important to understanding common pitfalls that may arise when posting such bail.

Sucked Into a Bad Deal

Most **Bail Bond Contracts generally require a financially solvent co-signer or indemnitor.** Personal Information detailing the co-signer as well as the defendant are traditionally required during the application process of a Bail Bond. Most documents for a standard Bail Bond contract include a promise to pay the Bail Bond in full and other cost if the defendant fails to appear in court. Other conditions may be placed on the defendant the riskier the Bond is. Bail Bond Companies are not Banks they do whatever is necessary to relive themselves of any financial burden resulting from a defendant.

Let's just say that a person fails to appear in court. When they fail to appear in court, a notice is sent to the bondsman from the court. He then has a date to appear in court to give account, reason or show cause to why the defendant failed to appear. In most of such contracts, there's a fee included for court appearances when the defendant fails to appear in court. If the defendant fails to appear or ran, the bail bondsman has to hire a bounty hunter, recovery agent, private investigator, or even conduct the service themselves. They'll incur cost on trying to locate the defendant. Those costs could be as high as 20% of the initial bail bond posted.

If the bond is $10,000 in a standard bail contract, a bondsman may charge you 20% of the bond plus the expenses if he has to try to locate the defendant, bring him back into custody, and all costs incurred in locating the defendant (meals, travel, gas, investigative services). This can get quite costly after the initial bail premium has been paid. When signing a bail bond, there are some heavy financial expenses to you. When signing for a bail bond, there are some heavy financial burden and responsibilities. If you're signing for someone you either do not know; do not have a relationship with, cannot locate, do not have any idea of what type of character traits they have, and who they are.

There have been many common pitfalls that people have fallen victim of when signing bail bonds. I've seen girlfriends who have only been dating a man for three months; the guy gets arrested on a grand larceny charge. He calls her from the jail. Next thing you know, she's signing a bail bond contract for $10,000. He disappears. He leaves her. He goes to another state. Now the bail bondsman is in legal proceedings with her, the co-signer or the indemnitor, for the surety and she is in litigation with thousands of dollars being garnished from her wages and pay.

Nobody works all his life to be involved in a deal like this. When signing a bail bond, be sure you know the person not just by name, not just by location, but by character, who they are as a person, what they represent, some of the everyday things that are going on in their life. You want to be able to help the bondsman locate this defendant and save you from any financial harm or devastation.

Shook Up on a $100,000 Bond

B ail fees and bond costs can be very, very expensive, sometimes as expensive as attorney fees that are mounting at an alarming rate, sometimes hourly or sometimes per appearance. Defendants who are charged with crimes can be in financial disaster when dealing with criminal charges. They panic and they have all kinds of burdens. As a co-signer or indemnitor for a bail bond, in normal bail bond terms, you have partnered with the defendant in this particular matter that they are dealing with, so you need to know who's handling the tab.

The tab can get expensive. Legal fees can be $5,000 upfront to maybe $10,000. Bail could be $20,000, so you would have to pay a bail premium of 10%, which is the standard industry rate in most cases (depending on the state) if bail is granted. For example, you may meet with your attorney before your warrant or you turn-in. You'll pay him an initial fee for his appearance or whatever you've arranged. He'll go into court, and after he goes to court the next thing that he'll do is to attend your arraignment. He may have to do a bond motion or a bond appeal or a couple of appearances on your behalf, and once he makes those appearances, a bail bond is set at what is traditionally called a bail review or a bail motion or a bond motion. You will then be granted bail.

If you are granted bail, bail could be upwards, on some serious charges, of $50,000, so then you would have to contact the bail bondsman, and a bail bondsman would post the bond for you. If you are rolling heavy in the cash, you may not have to worry about hiring a bail bondsman.

You may just want to take the $50,000 yourself and post it with the court. If the person fails to appear, it'd be no sweat, you've just lost $50,000. Most people just don't have that kind of money hanging around. With that being the case, you're already in the hole sometimes $7,000, $10,000.

I can remember one time when I posted bail for a gentleman, and the bond was $100,000. This was my first large bond that I ever posted. I was shaking in my boots when I went down to the jail to execute the bond. I'll never forget that day because, on that day, another bondsman saw me posting the bond, he said,

"Don't do it. He's going to run." It scared me and had me shaking in my boots. Immediately after that, I went, I sat down with his mom, girlfriend, family, and I sat down with everyone. I had a chance to get to know them, understand them, what was going on, who these people were. I had to get a fair assessment that I was entering into a contract with a person, and I was getting ready to put up $100,000, be on the hook and be responsible for that type of financial burden. I had to know who these people were, no different than they had to know who I was because they were giving me money.

I can remember they had to pay their lawyer $10,000, and then they turned back around and paid me $10,000. That's $20,000. This guy was not some corporate executive at a great company earning high six- figures. He was a guy that ran a lawn servicing business. He was a guy who sold cloth apparel part time. This might have been his savings. This might have been his family's savings. He still had a case that he was continuing to deal with, so he had to go to court. I remember when the case finally closed, the gentleman ended up fighting the case for almost two years. He eventually had to hire another lawyer. He had costs upon costs with restrictions and conditions to his bond.

When you're entering into legal matters and legal cases, depending on the seriousness of it and depending on how long it could be, be aware it could be a long road. A person could be out on bond one year, two years, or maybe even three years while pending a charge or waiting to go to trial.

CHAPTER

5

When Bail Causes a Change of Heart

They're possible pitfalls along the way. The arrest and release of a defendant are just one initial hill when trying to get somebody out of jail or dealing with a criminal matter with a friend or family member. The next day is the long journey ahead.

Most people are unaware of how cases may go or which direction that they may go in. Many times defendants are released from jail only to have their bond revoked, or they are charged with an additional crime arising from the same set of circumstances. All the costs and fees continue to mount and may burden or affect the friends and family members involved.

I have seen cases where bonds were set at ten thousand dollars, fifteen thousand dollars, twenty thousand dollars, even a hundred thousand dollars where the defendant made arrangements, hired an attorney, posted bail, and then, was subsequently released, only to have his bond revoked a week later, a day later, or two days. All the fees, all the costs that were initially paid seem wasted and sometimes, fees are still owed.

Many times defendants can request a bond reduction if it is difficult for the defendant and the family members to come up with bail amount and cost. They still have to pay their lawyer, they still may have remaining bail fees, and it can be quite stressful. Be aware when posting bail that a bail revocation is possible. The courts can do it, or the judge could do it.

Another common problem is when co-signers request for bail to be revoked. Relationships with friends, family members, or significant others can get toxic or change over time.

Mom and dad, boyfriend and girlfriend, distant relative or cousin, they no longer felt comfortable with dealing with the defendant and his issues. He was either on drugs, wasn't complying with what was asked in the home, wasn't doing what they were supposed to be doing as far as what the arrangements were, or sometimes, maybe it was a vindictive girlfriend who felt like, "Since I posted your bond, you better stay here and live with me and act right and be faithful to me."

There are a lot of conditions that can arise. I can remember one time when I got a phone call from a mom, and the mom said, "My son isn't acting right. Come pick him up."The problem was, this was a ten thousand dollar bond and this lady had not paid my full fee. She was asking me to come and revoke a bond and take a man back to jail, and she had not even committed or finished paying her initial fees. She didn't understand that if it cost me time and money to come out to have this gentleman picked up, that she will receive a bill from me for providing that service as well.

Posting bond is an important part of the legal process, it is critical that you pay attention to detail. That's why it is of vital importance to make sure that you know what you're signing, and know what you're paying. Bail revocation is one common pitfall along the road when posting bail.

Violated

There are many times when a defendant is arrested while out on bond from a previous bond or a previous legal situation. There are many times where defendants are charged with crimes, and they're already on probation. What ends up happening sometimes is whether it's a year later, two years later, three years later, they get arrested again for a new allegation.

When they get arrested for this new charge, they go through the full process of being released and going through the initial court appearances. Once that happens, next thing that you may encounter is the setting of a bond, and then a probation violation may be triggered. You may have a scenario where you have a friend or loved one or family member who had a recent run-in with the law and had a court obligation or probation in his sentencing which may have given him probation.

Let's say for example someone picks up a new charge of assault and battery. If previously convicted of the matter, a part of the sentencing was probation, therefore, a new allegation of assault and battery or any other allegation may trigger a probation violation. If he gets this probation violation, he'll have a hearing. When he has this initial hearing, there's a chance that he could be detained and placed back into custody while out on bond. Understand when you are signing for people, and you're getting people out of jail, be aware of their criminal history because sometimes there may be situations where they may trigger a probation violation, and they may be rearrested after you have already gotten them out of jail.

Surprise Notice

M any times, defendants have outstanding legal matters in another jurisdiction that need to be addressed. Many times, people are arrested, and they fail to appear in court while pending a case in another court. This can be very disastrous. I can remember scenarios where we have been in contact or assisted families in trying to get their loved one out of jail. They were arrested initially for a drug charge and then only to go through the process of getting a bail bond in that particular jurisdiction. A warrant pops up, either out of state or in-state or in the neighboring county for maybe a DWI. Now, they're in a scenario where they have a bond, the bond can be posted, but have outstanding legal matters in another jurisdiction that they have to go through the process. That can be very challenging to a family and a defendant.

As discussed earlier on mounting costs, sometimes you may have a lawyer in one county for one case, go through the process, and get a bond, only to be served a warrant for a charge and an arrest warrant or indictment in another county. Now you'll have to post your bond in that jurisdiction just to go to the other court to have that matter resolved. Sometimes, posting bond is advantageous because, as spoken earlier, legal issues can take very long times. When you're dealing with time, time is money. People are losing employment. People are getting behind on their bills. People are struggling with day-to-day living, with providing for their families. Legal matters can be very challenging so, sometimes, getting quick out of jail is the best route.

It's important that, when posting bond, you are aware of, not only the criminal history but also of the friend or family members' recent challenges or struggles with the law. Sometimes, that could prevent them from being released or trigger a warrant in a county in another state or another neighboring county before they can get out of jail. I've seen cases where a bond was $50,000 in one county and $50,000 in another, and then they may have another outstanding warrant in another state. They have all these bonds, they have all this cost, but they cannot be released. Very discouraging and very heartbreaking for a friend or family member or cosigner, so it is important that, before you sign the bail contract, assess what is ahead of you before spending your money.

Sometimes, I've had cases and scenarios where a gentleman had posted a bond with me, and the full premium had not been remitted. He had outstanding warrants in other counties, and family members were waiting for him to get out of jail and get a job. That doesn't work from a business standpoint. If you're a cosigner, you're an indemnitor, and sign for a bail bond, you have financial obligations to ensure that the contract is fulfilled. So, before you sign the bill, before you take on the responsibility, know that it's possible warrants could be out for the accused or the defendant's family or loved one that is dealing with the legal matter.

Free Only for a Minute

S ometimes one of the common pitfalls of being out on
bonds is that you can be arrested again. You've got one
charge in one county. You go through the process of being
arrested, being accused, and going to arraignment, appearing
before a judge, getting granted bail. You're released. You pay your
fees only to walk down the road in the next two, three, four, five
or six months to be charged again. This can be very devastating
because, as I spoke earlier, legal matters are very costly. Now
you have a pending case that you're currently dealing with, and
now have a new allegation that you've been charged with. It's
paramount, when signing for a co-defendant or a defendant with
a charge, that you are fully aware that if they are rearrested in
another jurisdiction and held without bail or there's a challenge
that may happen there, it could trigger a bond revocation in the
other jurisdiction, or this charge could be much more serious
when they fail to appear, and they're not able to attend court

hearings for their ongoing matter.

It is paramount that you know the whereabouts of the defendant at all times and what's going on in his life. Sometimes we have people that just have a string of bad luck, and they get arrested multiple times. Often for unknown reasons. Sometimes it's the system. Sometimes it's the people. Understand that these are possible scenarios that you could encounter when posting bond. I've gotten calls at times from family members and friends, who posted bond three months prior, only to call me back this time and say, "I'm not going to do it this time." Why? "He's not living right. He's not acting right. He has not been treating me right." Whatever the scenario or whatever the circumstance, they decline to post bond or provide assistance for the defendant. Sometimes they even ask for the other bond to be revoked. Understand that when dealing with a legal matter, it's lengthy, and it is possible that the defendant could be arrested or rearrested again for the same charge or a new allegation in another jurisdiction.

Addition Could Mean Subtraction

S ometimes when released out on bail after paying costs, you may have more conditions to your bond, like pre-trial services that you may have to abide by, or you may have a condition of the court while the case is still pending and the matter is still outstanding. There have been times when bonds are set, and alcohol monitoring is required. There have been times where bonds are set to where an individual has to check in with the pre-trial services officer while the case is on-going and they may be required to attend these meetings at specified dates and times. When conditions are violated, it now puts the defendant at risk. At risk to have his bond revoked, or pick up a new subsequent matter of pre-trial service violation or bail violation, so understand that right now or in the moment that you are making the decision to get someone out on bail, know that they may have additional conditions that may be required.

Make sure you speak to your attorney and make sure that those conditions are clear, and you're following all the directives of the court and the requirement of the bond. Having your bail revoked after paying hundreds or even thousands of dollars to get out is very disheartening to a defendant or a family member due to the severity of the financial obligations, so it's important that when you are released that you make sure you understand the conditions of your bond.

CHAPTER

10

A Choice Between the Wife and the Girlfriend

Many times, when a defendant is charged with a crime, they panic. They call their mother, father, aunt, uncle, and their cousin. They're desperate to get anybody who will try to get them out. Essentially, what happens is, they alert and alarm all of these people, so everybody is trying to come up with different ways and resources, to try to have the Defendant released. I've seen cases and scenarios in my career, where a gentleman one time in particular had a wife and a girlfriend. He called his wife to help him out and also called his girlfriend to help him out. I arrived at the Jail to post the bond, and I happened to be working with the girlfriend. Another Bondsman got a phone call on the same defendant, and he was with the wife. I was sitting in the lobby; I posted the Bond. The other bondsman wanted to make a stink about it because he had the wife. Either way it goes, we ended up conducting the Service. Upon conducting the service, and the defendant being released, he walked outside only to see his girlfriend and his wife in the same lobby.

What a disaster! Being arrested, and then having relationship difficulties within your marriage. That's something you don't want to do. When trying to post bail, try to gather as much information and resources from the defendant, as well as other family members, or those close to the defendant, before trying to make arrangements to get them out. Sometimes you have families that call multiple Bail bonding companies, or multiple Lawyers, so you have two lawyers going down to visit the same defendant, or you have two bail bonding companies trying to post bond for the same defendant. It can be a nightmare, so think fast, and think smart. Next time a friend, or loved one calls you, make sure you gather all the information about the arrest, where it took place, who's willing to help, who has resources to pledge, and who is going to sign off on all documents, and being responsible for assisting and helping the defendant? It makes life smoother. It makes the process easier, and it avoids problems that may incur upon the release of the accused.

Track Stars

There are many times when a defendant is incarcerated, and they know that they have time hanging over their heads. That means that upon conviction, or an allegation, they are looking at backup time from previous charges. What generally happens is that they look for the next family member, friend, or even bondsman to get them out of jail, with a false promise, only to get cold feet and take off. There are many times in my recent past where a defendant was charged with a crime, had a significant bond, called every bond company in town, and one Bondsman happened to get him out with no money down, and the guy took off, after leading him into a backyard, where he stated that he had money stored.

You have many people that are involved in the criminal justice system that know the ins and outs of it very well, so you, as a Co-Signer, Indemnitor or even a Bondsman, need to be mindful of the individuals that you are involved with, and that you're posting bond for. Next time you get that call, make sure that the defendant is not facing significant backup time. These could lead to him being released, then on the run for the next two to three years, and you being left holding the bag as to surety with a co-Signer, who is left at risk of a lawsuit, and losing tons of money for posting bail.

Five Most Important Questions You Must Ask

I t's important that when entering into a bail bond contract you are fully aware of what you are signing and what you are doing. Bail bond contracts have broken up families and caused tremendous financial problems. This book was written to help you, the cosigner or the family member come to a very prudent decision. When you decide to make the choice or you get a phone call, or happen to drive up to jail, beware of the pitfalls that you could encounter.

Ensure you ask all the right questions and if possible, contact an attorney and make sure that you get sufficient legal advice to answer all your questions and ease your comfort during these emotional times. Emotions sometimes can cause us as people to make very poor decisions. Before you sign for a bond, make sure that you've thought about the key points listed in this book.

I know in recent past you have seen reality TV shows on bail. Sometimes it can be entertaining. It's fun, but in reality, this is a real business. Bail is not a game. It's a good business, and there are good agents out there that are providing this service to the community to help those who are involved in the criminal justice system that is facing heartache, pain, and sometimes despair. Before you enter into a bail contract, follow the checklist I have listed below to save you time, money, stress, and of course, blood pressure. There are many times when I have been in contact with family members who lost their lives due to stress over these circumstances.

You will need to check off the checklist below before you decide to make that decision to get somebody out of jail.

If you can answer the above five questions with clarity, with detail, self-awareness, you can come to a quality decision before you post bail.

1. How well am I familiar with the defendant?
2. What are the terms, my cost?
3. What are the facts and the allegations the defendant is facing?
4. Does the defendant have other criminal charges?
5. Am I committed for the right reasons in helping the defendant?

For further insight, questions, or concerns, please feel free to reach out to us. We will be glad to help you in assisting you in having your loved one released from jail.

Glossary

Bail Bond
   (Law) a document in which a prisoner and one or more sureties guarantee that the prisoner will attend the court hearing of the charge against him if he is released on bail

Appeal
   A. higher court's review of the correctness of a decision by a lower court.
   B. A case so reviewed.
   C. A request for a higher court to review the decision of a lower court.

Arraignment
   After the arrest, booking, and initial bail phases of the criminal process, the first stage of courtroom-based proceedings takes place.

Bail Hearing
   To determine what is necessary to ensure a defendant's appearance at trial, a judge or magistrate examines the nature and circumstances of the charges, with particular attention to whether the offense involves violence or narcotic drugs. The court may inquire into the nature and value of any property that might be offered as collateral. The court also examines the weight of the evidence against the defendant, whether the person was on parole or probation at the time of the present arrest, the nature and seriousness of danger to others in the community.

Appendix

Sample generic bail agreement forms

PLAIN TALK CONTRACT

Contract Date: _____

Power No: _____

Bond Amount: _____

Premium Amount: _____

*** The English version of this form is the official version. The Spanish language form is for informational purposes only ***
La versión inglés de esta forma es la versión oficial. La forma en lenguaje español es para propósitos informativos únicamente.

I understand that signing this bond for obtaining the release of defendant _____, I am responsible for him/her appearing in Court each time he/she is so ordered; also if he/she fails to follow any and all instructions or orders of the Court or forfeits this bond, and it becomes necessary to apprehend and surrender him/her to the Court, I understand that I am responsible for any and all expenses incurred as a result of such forfeiture occurs and the defendant is not surrendered to the Court within the time prescribed by law, I understand that I am required to pay the FULL AMOUNT of the bond posted, including any unpaid bail premium. Further, that immediately upon such forfeiture and non-cash collateral, including real estate, may be immediately converted to cash sufficient to cover the bond amount.

I further understand that the premium owing and/or paid on this bond is fully earned upon the filing of this bond. The fact that the defendant may have been improperly arrested, or his/her bail reduced, or his/her case dismissed, shall not obligate the return or forgiveness of any portion of the premium.

IMPORTANT NOTICE:

There is a waiting period of approximately 30 days from the date the bond is exonerated before collateral can be returned. We MUST receive written notice from the Clerk of Court before return collateral can be returned.

I am not a paid signer. I have no connection with/to a Bail Bond Consultant. I have read the above contract and understand it, agree to fulfill ALL of the provisions herein and am bound by all the terms and conditions of all documents signed.

Signed: _____
Defendant Signature

_____
Indemnitor Signature

_____
Indemnitor Signature

Agent: _____

WN-0110 (8/10)

RECORDING REQUESTED BY:

AND WHEN RECORDED MAIL TO:

SPACE ABOVE THIS LINE FOR RECORDER'S USE

DEED OF TRUST

*** The English version of this form is the official version. The Spanish language form is for informational purposes only. ***
La versión inglés de esta forma es la versión oficial. La forma en lenguaje español es para propósitos informativos únicamente.

BOND NO.

DEFENDANT

THIS DEED OF TRUST, made this _____ day of _____, _____, between _____ herein called TRUSTOR, and UNIVERSAL FIRE CASUALTY INSURANCE COMPANY herein called TRUSTEE, and WILLIAMSBURG NATIONAL INSURANCE COMPANY herein called BENEFICIARY, WITNESSETH: That Trustor hereby GRANTS to TRUSTEE IN TRUST, WITH POWER OF SALE, all that property in the County of _____ in the state of _____, described as:

Lot: _____ Block: _____ Tract: _____ APN: _____

as per map recorded in Book _____ Page _____ of Maps, Official Records in the office of the

County Recorder of _____ County.

Commonly known as _____

FOR THE PURPOSES OF SECURING payment to the said Beneficiary of the monies due to and all of losses, damages, expenditures and liability suffered, sustained, made or incurred by WILLIAMSBURG NATIONAL INSURANCE COMPANY, hereinafter called the Surety or Beneficiary (and as more fully set forth and described in a certain Bail Bond Agreement, which agreement is made a part hereof by reference as though herein full set forth) on account of, growing out of, or resulting from the execution of a certain bond on behalf of _____ in the matter of _____ vs. _____ AND FOR WHICH AMOUNTS and the matter set forth in the said indemnity agreement, are security. (Power No. _____).

IS AGREED AND CONDITIONED that a certificate signed by the Beneficiary at any time hereafter setting forth that the said bond has been declared forfeited or that a loss, damage, expenditure or liability has been sustained by the Surety or Beneficiary on account of the aforesaid Undertaking; the date(s) and amount(s) of such loss, damages, expenditures and/or liability; that payment has been demanded of the party of the parties on whose behalf the aforesaid Undertaking has or is about to be executed; and that such loss, damages, expenditures or determined liability has not been paid to the Beneficiary, shall be conclusive and binding on the Trustor, and shall be the warrant of the Trustee to proceed forthwith to foreclose and sell upon the security herein, and from the proceeds of sale (after deducting expenses including cost and search of evidence of title) pay to the Beneficiary the amount so certified, including interest at the highest legal rate per month from demand to date of payment and attorney fees.

IT IS FURTHER AGREED THAT: Upon delivery of said Certificate to the Trustee, the Beneficiary may declare all sums or obligations secured hereby due and payable by delivery to the Trustee of written declaration of default and demand for sale and of written notice of default and of election to cause to be sold said property, which notice the Trustee shall cause to be duly filed for record.

IT SHALL BE DEEMED SUFFICIENT if proceedings to foreclose and sell the security herein are executed by any one of the above-named Trustees and it shall be deemed sufficient if a full reconveyance is executed by any one of the above-named Trustees; and said one Trustee shall be deemed to be the attorney-in-fact for the other Trustees for those purposes. The authority thus granted herein shall be deemed to be coupled with an interest and shall not be affected by the death or incompetency of any of the Trustees for whom such one Trustee shall be acting.

THE UNDERSIGNED TRUSTOR REQUESTS that a copy of any notice of default and of any notice of sale hereunder be mailed to him/her at his/her mailing address opposite his/her signature hereto. Failure to insert such address shall be deemed a waiver for a copy of such notice.

SIGNATURE OF TRUSTOR	STREET AND NUMBER	CITY	STATE	ZIP CODE

STATE OF _____

COUNTY OF _____ } s.s.

Subscribed and sworn to (or affirmed) before me on this _____, day of _____, 20 _____,

by _____ proved to me on the basis of satisfactory evidence to be the person(s) who appeared before me.

(Seal)

Signature _____

WN-0116-(9/11)

APPLICATION AND AGREEMENT FOR SURETY BAIL BOND

Indemnity Agreement

*** The English version of this form is the official version. The Spanish language form is for informational purposes only.***
*** La versión englés de esta forma es la versión oficial. La forma en lenguaje español es para propósitos informativos únicamente.***

WHEREAS, the undersigned, hereinafter called the First Party, whether one or more, have made or do now make application to _____ hereinafter called the Second Party, to have executed or secured the execution by Williamsburg National Insurance Company, a corporation, hereinafter called the Surety, of a Bail Bond in the penal sum of $ _____ on behalf of _____ hereinafter called the Defendant, and

WHEREAS, with the express understanding and condition that this Agreement would be executed by the First Party, the Second Party has arranged for the execution of said Bail Bond or does hereby agree to arrange for the execution of the same.

NOW, THEREFORE, in consideration of the Second Party arranging for the execution of the Bail Bond aforementioned, or in the event that said Bail Bond shall already have been executed and the Defendant released from custody thereon, then in consideration of the Second Party causing the Surety to permit the Defendant to remain for the time being free from the custody of the Court under said Bail Bond, the First Party and each of them do hereby jointly and severally agree and promise as follows:

FIRST
TO PAY TO THE SECOND PARTY THE SUM OF $ _____ as fully earned premium for the execution of said Bail Bond and, unless prohibited by law, a like sum annually in advance each year hereafter until the Surety shall be legally discharged from all the liability thereunder. The fact that the Defendant may have been improperly taken into custody or his bail reduced, or his/her cause dismissed forthwith shall not obligate the Second Party to waive or return said premium or any portion thereof.

SECOND
To indemnify and to at all times save harmless the Second Party and the Surety from and against any and all liability, demands, expenses attorney fees, debts, damages, judgments, or losses of every kind, character or nature the Second Party or the Surety shall at any time or for any cause sustain, by reason of the execution or the arranging or obtaining the execution of the Bail Bond aforementioned or any renewal thereof or any bond issued in continuance thereof or as a substitute therefore. To pay to the Second Party or the Surety immediately upon demand the penal amount of said Bail Bond whenever the Second Party or the Surety deems such payment necessary for protection, upon any change of condition which increase the hazard, which sum shall be retained and used by the Second Party and the Surety as security hereunder. TO PAY TO THE SECOND PARTY AND THE SURETY IMMEDIATELY UPON THE DECLARATION OF FORFEITURE OF SAID BAIL BOND THE PENAL AMOUNT THREOF AND NOT IN ANY WAY PREVENT THE SECOND PARTY OR THE SURETY FROM THEREUPON PROCEEDING TO CONVERT ANY NON-CASH SECURITY HELD TO CASH SUFFICIENT TO SATISFY THE BOND AMOUNT.

THIRD
To aid and cooperate with the Second Party and the Surety in securing exoneration of the Second Party and the Surety from any and all liability under said Bail Bond, including the surrender of the Defendant to the custody of the Court should the Second Party or the Surety deem such action necessary or advisable, even though such surrender may have been made before the Bail Bond is forfeited or any liability incurred thereon. No obligation shall exist on the part of the Second Party or the Surety to return or waive the premium or any portion thereof, except as may be otherwise required by law or the rules of the Insurance Commissioner.

FOURTH
To reimburse the Second Party and/or Surety for the actual expenses incurred and caused by a breach by the Defendant of any of the terms for which the application and Bail Bond were written not in excess of the penal amount of the Bail Bond including all expenses or liabilities incurred as a result of searching for, recapturing or returning the Defendant to custody, incurred by the Second Party or the Surety as necessary in apprehending or endeavoring to apprehend the Defendant, including legal fees incurred by the Second Party or the Surety in making application to a court for an order to vacate or to set aside the order of forfeiture or summary judgment entered thereon unless otherwise required by applicable law (if any) as stated in an attached addendum. All money owing to the Second Party, pursuant to this Agreement, that is in arrears for a period of 30 days, shall accrue monthly at the highest legal rate of interest. Additionally, the First Party hereby authorizes the Second Party to conduct a credit check and other financial inquiries on the First Party.

FIFTH
The undersigned agree that these obligations apply to all other Bail Bonds executed for the same charge for which the above mentioned Bail Bond was executed, or any charge arising out of the same act or occurrence, regardless of whether said Bail Bonds are filed before or after conviction, but not in a greater amount.

SIXTH
That all money or other property which the First Party has deposited or may deposit with the Second Party or the Surety may be applied as collateral security or indemnity for matters contained herein, and to accomplish the purposes contained herein, the Second Party and/or the Surety is authorized to lawfully levy upon said collateral in the manner provided by law and to apply the proceeds therefrom and any and all money deposited to payment of a reimbursement for the hereinabove liabilities, losses, costs, damages and expenses. If collateral received by the Second Party is in excess of the bail forfeited, such excess shall be returned to the depositor immediately upon the application of the collateral to the forfeiture, subject to any claim of the Second Party and the Surety for unpaid premium or the hereinabove charges.

SEVENTH
To pay the Second Party and the Surety's attorney fees in the event of suit hereunder for breach of this Agreement incurred by the Second Party or the Surety under this Agreement.

EIGHTH
In making application for the hereinabove described Bail Bond we warrant all of the statements made on the reverse of this page to be true and we agree to advise the Second Party or the Surety of any change (especially change of address) within 48 hours after such change has occurred and agree that any failure to so notify shall be cause for the immediate surrender of the Defendant and in such event no premium shall be subject to return.

NINTH
If any provision or provisions of this instrument are deemed void or unenforceable under the law of any jurisdiction governing its construction or enforcement, this instrument shall not be void or vitiated thereby but shall be construed and enforced with the same effect as though such provision or provisions were omitted.

TENTH
You agree that Surety may attach a location tracking device on any vehicle driven by you, at any time, without notice, and monitor through any available technology. You further agree that Surety may use location technologies to locate your wireless device at any time during the period of Defendant's bail and any applicable remission period, and the Bond is conditioned upon your full compliance with the following terms and conditions: (i) Surety, at its discretion, will use network-based location technologies to find you; (ii) this is the only notice you will receive for the collection of your location information; (iii) Surety will retain location data only while the Bond is in force and during any applicable remission period; (iv) Surety will disclose location information only to the courts as required by court order; (v) Surety and its licensed producers, designees and representatives will be the only persons with access to your location information; (vi) YOU WILL NOT HAVE THE OPTION TO OPT-OUT OF LOCATION USE DURING THE BAIL PERIOD; and (vii) all questions relating to location capability should be directed to Surety.

ELEVENTH
That these covenants shall be binding not only upon us, jointly and severally, but as well upon our respective heirs, executors, administrators, successors and assigns.

IN WITNESS WHEREOF THE UNDERSIGNED DO HEREBY ACKNOWLEDGE RECEIPT OF THE FOREGOING AGREEMENT AND VERILY STATE THAT THEY AND EACH OF THEM HAVE CAREFULLY READ THE SAME AND UNDERSTAND THE CONTENTS THEREOF and do now set

their hand this _____ day of _____, 20_____.

Defendant Signature	Print Name			S.S. Number
Address	City	Zip Code	Cell Phone	Home Phone
Indemnitor Signature	Print Name			S.S. Number
Address	City	Zip Code	Cell Phone	Home Phone
Indemnitor Signature	Print Name			S.S. Number
Address	City	Zip Code	Cell Phone	Home Phone

INDEMNITOR/GUARANTOR CHECK LIST

DATE _____ BAIL AMOUNT $ _____

DEFENDANT _____ PREMIUM AMOUNT $ _____

JAIL _____ AMOUNT PAID DOWN $ _____

BAIL BOND # _____ CASH COLLATERAL $ _____

1. I have read and received a copy of the standard Williamsburg National Insurance Company Indemnity Agreement for surety bail bond.

2. This indemnitor/guarantor checklist is intended to clarify and explain the standard Williamsburg National Insurance Company Agreement for surety bail bond.

3. I understand I am responsible to make the payments for money due on the premium as described above. Finance charges are computed on unpaid balances on the 30th day of each month at the rate of _____ percent per annum. There is a _____ percent late fee on all scheduled payments not received within five days of the due date. (Note: The insurance company is not a party to any premium financing. Any financial agreement is strictly between the bail agent/agency and indemnitor.

4. I understand I am required to pay the amount of the bail premium every year, in advance hereafter, until the surety is legally discharged from all liability on the bonds posted. (States with Renewable Premiums).

5. A forfeiture of the bail will be entered by the court if the defendant fails to make any court appearance. I understand that if the bond is ordered forfeited and it is not ordered reinstated, or exonerated within the time allowed by law, that I must pay the full amount of the bail forfeited plus expenses to the bail agent/agency.

6. I understand I am responsible if it becomes necessary to arrest and surrender the defendant and that I am responsible for paying all reasonable costs incurred for locating, apprehending, transporting and surrendering the defendant to custody. Investigation costs will begin to accrue after a court forfeiture or when any co-signer requests the defendant be placed back in custody or when any condition exists as defined in the bail bond agreement. If no investigation costs have been incurred prior to a voluntary surrender of defendant at the jail facility of the court specified on the bail receipt there will be no investigation cost charged. Reasonable court costs, as described in Paragraph 7 of the checklist, will be charged if applicable and a receipt will be provided.

7. I understand that if the bail is ordered forfeited by the court, that I am responsible to pay court costs and reasonable appearance or attorney's fees (a minimum of $ _____) for the bail agent to reinstate or exonerate the bail bond if necessary.

8. I understand that if I breach the bail bond agreement, by non payment or any other action as defined by the bail agreement, I am responsible for any collection actions taken, including attorneys fees and costs.

9. I understand that my collateral cannot be released until all bonds posted on my behalf for defendant have been exonerated and written notice from the court received by the bail agency.

10. I understand that substitution of collateral is done at the discretion of the surety and the bail bonding agency. There are no agreements to substitute collateral at a future date.

11. I understand that it is my responsibility to request return of any collateral provided. There may be a delay of return of collateral until the bail agency has researched the exoneration date and verified the bail bond status with the appropriate courts. This process may be done faster if I obtain written verification of the bond exoneration from the court and provide it to the bail agency.

12. This checklist is intended to explain and clarify the standard Williamsburg National Insurance Company Agreement for Surety Bail, which is the entire contract with the bail agency. I understand that there are no additional terms nor are there any exemptions to the contract, either in writing or verbally, that limit my responsibility under the bail agreement.

13. I declare that all statements made on the application and financial statement are true. I agree to notify the bail agency, within 48 hours of any changes, including but not limited to any change of address, or employment of either myself or the criminal defendant

14. I understand the obligations under this agreement are joint and several. This means that I may be held solely and individually liable for up to the full amount owed for any and all charges, even if there are other cosigners on the agreement.

15. Agreement of Venue: I agree that if legal action between the parties concerning this bail bond is brought, it shall be brought in and before a federal or state court in _____ and in the State of _____ .

I HAVE READ, UNDERSTAND AND AGREE WITH THE ABOVE TERMS.

SIGNATURE: _____   SIGNATURE: _____

NAME (print): _____   NAME (print): _____

RECEIVED COPY: _____

WN-11019 (08/10)

THE BAIL BONDS PROCESS
THE DEFINITIVE STEP BY STEP GUIDE

1. Criminal Allegation / or Complaint

2. Police / Law Enforcement Contact

3. Physical Arrest

4. Appearance Before Magistrate / Commissioner

5. Bail review secured, unsecured bail. Held without bail.

6. Defendant Phone Call Family, Attorney, Bondsmen

7. Booking

8. Pre-trial interview

9. Arraignment with Judge - Bail Review

10. Defendant hires or gets appointed attorney if qualified

11. Bond Motion

12. Bond Appeal

13. Preliminary Hearing

14. Bond Motion to Reconsider

15. Bail Contract Signed

16. Bond Posted at Jail

17. Defendant Released - unless detainees in other jurisdictions

18. Defendant attends all court dates until court case is completed.

The Cost of Bail By State

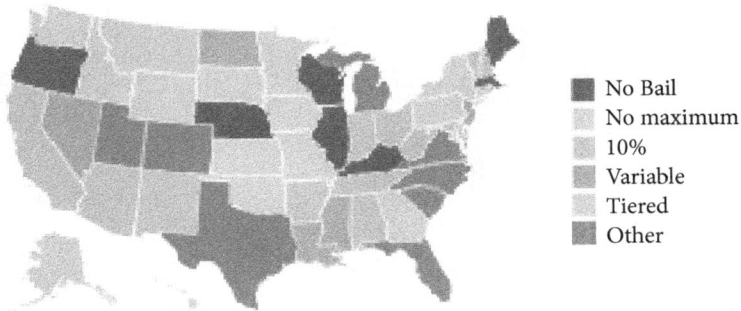

- No Bail
- No maximum
- 10%
- Variable
- Tiered
- Other

To learn more about the cost of bail by state visit:

https://www.aboutbail.com/pages/bail-cost